Original title:
Eucalyptus Elegy

Copyright © 2025 Creative Arts Management OÜ
All rights reserved.

Author: Colin Leclair
ISBN HARDBACK: 978-1-80566-775-9
ISBN PAPERBACK: 978-1-80566-795-7

Nostalgic Canopy

Beneath the leaves, I reminisce,
A squirrel scolds, can't let me miss.
With whispers sweet in the warm sunlight,
I search for my sandwich, an embarrassing sight.

Branches dance as I sway and sway,
Tickled by breezes that laugh and play.
Memories linger, a cheeky breeze,
Shaking old branches, inviting some tease.

Soliloquy of the Strands

A tree trunk talks to a raccoon near,
Sharing gossip over fresh green beer.
'Why sniff the air?' the raccoon replies,
'When the chips fall, I'll eat all the fries.'

Roots stretch out for a long embrace,
While worms and ants plot saving grace.
But trees are wise with their sitting pose,
Watching lovers fight then make up with prose.

Secrets in the Shade

In the shade where whispers collide,
A secret mission, with squirrels I glide.
The acorn heist, oh, what a crime!
While birds just chirp, saying, 'It's not time!'

Sunbeams tickle, making shadows play,
While ants march on in a perfect array.
Echoes of laughter from a nearby crew,
As I trip on roots—it's a real zoo!

The Horizon Through the Trees

Through branches wide, I make my peek,
A world so vast, I feel quite chic.
But wait, who's that with a picnic basket?
To their peanut butter, I might just fasten!

The horizon smiles as clouds drift near,
While laughter escapes like a true frontier.
Yet gravity's lure makes me miss a step,
'Tree roots are tricky,' I silently pep.

Remnants of Rustling Leaves

The trees tell tales with their creaks,
They gossip while the sunlight sneaks,
A squirrel laughs, it's quite a show,
As leaves fall softly, go with the flow.

The branches wiggle with a bit of sass,
Who knew such wisdom comes with grass?
A breezy dance with a twist and shout,
Who knew trees had such a clout?

Roots play poker, what a sight!
The canopy stands, oh so polite.
Birds come by to join the game,
Cackling loud, without a shame.

So if you walk beneath the boughs,
Listen closely, take a bow.
There's humor in the rustling rust,
In every leaf, there's joy and trust.

Glistening Raindrops

Raindrops bounce, a little chorus,
On leafy hats, they make a fuss.
They tumble down like little beads,
Quenching thirst for all the needs.

Puddles gather, a mirror bliss,
Reflecting clouds with a squishy kiss.
The trees wear diamonds, quite the show,
Waltzing gently in puddle flow.

A playful breeze joins in the game,
Whirling drops, oh what a claim!
They giggle softly on the ground,
Watering thoughts, profound yet sound.

So let it rain, let spirits lift,
Nature's humor, the ultimate gift.
With every drop, a jest does bloom,
In glistening pearls, there's no room for gloom.

Sorrow Among the Branches

In the shade, an old tree sighs,
Telling stories, under cloudy skies.
With leaves that flutter, just for fun,
Spilling secrets when day is done.

An acorn fell and missed its mark,
Dreams of growing tall and stark.
Yet here it lies, all tucked away,
In leafy laughter, come what may.

Birds mock the branches as they sway,
"Cheer up!" they chirp, "It's just a day!"
Life's too short for gloomy faces,
Join the dance, in wild embraces.

So let the branches hold your tears,
In glimmers of joy through the years.
For even sorrow must take a bow,
In this tree's tale, laugh with me now.

Sighs of the Old Grove

The old grove grumbles, quite a sound,
Moaning wisdom that's profound.
With whispers strong in the evening breeze,
It raises brows, and some unease.

"Oh, the weight!" it says with flair,
"Beneath this bark, there's wisdom rare."
But nearby, a beetle rolls his eyes,
"Chill out, old friend, it's just the skies!"

A woodpecker drums a silly beat,
Echoes bounce from root to seat.
The trees respond with rustling laughs,
Joining in on the wacky halves.

So raise a glass to roots and shoots,
For giggles bloom in leafy boots.
In every sigh, there's humor stowed,
In the old grove's heart, let joy be flowed.

Memories Wrapped in Green

In the shade of leaves so wide,
We laugh as branches seem to hide.
Squirrels dance in silly glee,
Chasing dreams up the old tree.

With each rustle, secrets spill,
Stories shared give such a thrill.
Nature's quirks, they make us smile,
A leafy jest goes on awhile.

Eulogy to the Timeless Canopy

Oh, mighty giants, standing tall,
You've seen it all, the rise and fall.
Your bark like armor, wise and bold,
Quite the gossip, always told.

In your branches, tales abound,
From acorns tossed to silent sound.
You crack a joke, we all chime in,
Life's playful dance where laughs begin.

The Forest's Quiet Farewell

When the time comes for goodbyes,
Leaves don their coats, disguise the cries.
Gentle breezes whisper fun,
While shadows play, the day is done.

Roots deep in soil, they just won't budge,
Yet the trees give a cheeky nudge.
With every sway and creaky moan,
They chuckle softly, 'You're not alone!'

Wisps of Life's Abiding Breath

In the stillness, chuckles rise,
As branches sway, in sweet surprise.
Leaves wave gently, a farewell show,
Nature giggles, 'It's time to go!'

Whispers linger in morning dew,
Trees crack a joke just for you.
With every breeze, their spirit sings,
Life's a jest, and joy it brings.

Shadows of a Wistful Branch

In the breeze, a branch sways,
Whispering tales of lazy days.
Leaves giggle in the bright sun,
While squirrels plot their next fun.

Roots are tangled in a dance,
As ladies' hats take on a chance.
A shadow casts on the ground,
Where lost shoes can often be found.

The sky winks with a cheeky grin,
As birds parade, one by one, in.
A twist of fate, a twist of vine,
Nature laughs, it's all so fine.

So here we bask, in grassy patches,
Where laughter's carried in delightful batches.
With every breeze, a secret shared,
In the realm of branches, none are scared.

The Boughs Remember

Once a bough held dreams so tall,
Now it's just a seat for all.
A picnic feast, beneath its shade,
With crumbs for ants, this bond we've made.

Echoes of laughter, they cling tight,
As boughs sway gently, day and night.
Each ring a tale of whimsy spun,
Shuffling leaves, oh what fun!

Naughty winds play pranks galore,
Tickling the leaves as they explore.
Branches bow as if they know,
The secrets of every breeze that blows.

In every rustle, joy abounds,
Nature's jokes are all around.
The boughs remember, with flair and jest,
In this grove, we are truly blessed.

Faded Fragrance of Forgotten Days

Once bright blooms have now grown shy,
Petals drift like dreams that fly.
Yet soft scents linger in the air,
A fragrant laugh, a gentle dare.

Old branches creak like ancient jokes,
Whispering tales of prankish folks.
With every breeze, a chuckle's found,
As echoes flutter all around.

Leaves murmur secrets of time gone past,
Crafty memories that still hold fast.
In the twilight, they wink and sway,
Sorting through the mischief of yesterday.

Now the flowers fade, but hearts expand,
For in their silence, jokes still stand.
Faded fragrance, yet spirits bright,
In nature's jest, we find delight.

Reverie in Rustic Green

In the heart of tranquil scenes,
Lies a world, all dressed in green.
Trees twirl like they know a dance,
With leaves that tease and branches prance.

Sunlight tickles the grassy floor,
Where bunnies hop, and laughter soars.
Yet, hidden there, an old shoe rests,
A relic of weird, forgotten quests.

Nestled in a gnarled embrace,
Funny creatures share their space.
A chorus of chirps, oh what a show,
While chipmunks steal the seeds below.

In rustic realms, where nature plays,
There's a joke for all in life's charades.
So rest a while, let laughter glean,
In the reverie of rustic green.

Unraveling in the Underbrush

In the grove where the leaves twirl,
Squirrels dance, causing quite a whirl.
A koala snores without a care,
While a lizard gives me a curious stare.

Bumblebees buzz with a silly hum,
Snakes sneak by, feeling quite glum.
They eye the tree for their shade parade,
But the winds laugh, and they start to fade.

Unraveled roots twist and shout,
They pull at shoes as I wander about.
Who knew the ground could be so sly?
Maybe I'll just tiptoe by.

But oh, the bark laughs with such delight,
As I tumble down, wings taking flight.
Nature's pranksters join the cheer,
In underbrush tales, there's always a leer.

Chasing the Clouds

I once chased a cloud on a lark,
Thought I could catch it, oh what a spark!
It fluffed up like a pillow, so bright,
Then zoomed away, giving me a fright.

The humor of nature, a grand ol' show,
A gust of wind made my hat blow.
Just like that cloud, it danced on high,
While I stood below, shouting, "Oh my!"

With each puffy form, I fancied a game,
An elephant here, a duck with a name.
But alas, as the sun dipped low,
They morph into nothing, just so you know.

Yet I giggle with glee, all in good fun,
Chasing the sunset to greet the night's run.
In the fading light, my dreams drift too,
A cloud-chaser's life—just a whim, who knew?

Lingering Last Light

As the sun dips low, shadows prance,
Crickets chirp, and the fireflies dance.
The last light chuckles at the day's end,
A playful wink, like an old friend.

Leaves wave goodbye, in comical glee,
Nature's stage, where all can see.
In the theater of dusk, the stars dress right,
And wink at the moon with all their might.

In this whimsical twilight, don't be shy,
Join the laughter beneath the sky.
For every critter has a tale to drop,
In the fading glow, the giggles don't stop.

So linger a while, soak up the jest,
As day turns to night, and all finds rest.
In this dance of light, both funny and bright,
We'll sway with the evening, till morning's first light.

Sighs of the Aromatic Forest

In the forest where scents collide,
A koala laughs, swinging with pride.
Leaves tickle noses, laughter does swell,
Even the branches seem to yell!

Breeze carries giggles, a playful tease,
Squirrels dance up, down, through the trees.
Nature's joke, a comical spree,
Whispers of joy, wild jubilee!

Beneath the Canopy of Memory

Under leafy hats, we recall the days,
When grasshoppers hopped in curious ways.
Every rustle tells tales, absurd,
Of a wise old owl and his crazy bird.

Raccoons in suits lounge by the stream,
Debating their next big scheme.
The branches chuckle, sharing their gossip,
Nature's comedy, a colorful flip!

The Lament of Leaf and Bark

Oh, the woes of those leafy friends,
Bickering over where sunlight ends.
A maple boasts, 'I'm quite the star!'
While birches sigh, 'You're not so far!'

Gnarled roots stomp in protest loud,
As they attempt to form a crowd.
Nature's squabble, a hilarious scene,
As shadows slide in, ever so keen!

Echoes in the Scented Breeze

In the breeze, whispers float and play,
Calm puffs carrying jokes from yesterday.
The flowers giggle, petals all aglow,
They joined in on a funny show!

Marshmallows drifting on a sweet perfume,
While trees sway along, making room.
Each echo a chuckle, a light-hearted jest,
In this fragrant world, we're truly blessed!

Beneath Clouded Skies

Beneath a gray and moody dome,
The leaves dance like they're stuck at home.
The branches bend and shake with glee,
They're chatting gossip about the bee.

A kookaburra's laugh begins to rise,
While munching on some snack supplies.
The wind whispers secrets, oh so sly,
As clouds pout like they've lost a pie.

Chirping crickets play a tune so hearty,
While some shy lizard joins the party.
With every rustle, a wild jest,
That's enough to give the trees some rest.

So beneath these skies that threaten rain,
Life dances to the rhythm of absurd gain.
For every gloom, there's humor near,
In nature's sketchbook, laughter's clear.

Melancholy at Dusk

At dusk, the shadows stretch and yawn,
Leaves stretch their limbs, saying 'C'mon!'.
The sunset glows in purple hues,
While birds eye the sky for food reviews.

A kangaroo with elegance hops by,
Suddenly trips, oh my, oh my!
The moon giggles as it begins to peak,
While trees roll their eyes at the chaos peak.

The evening flirts with nervous light,
As crickets practice for the night flight.
A sly possum steals a snack with flair,
"I'll share!" it says—then gives a glare.

But as the dusk whispers its last,
Nature chuckles, forgetting the past.
Under this whimsy-filled twilight sphere,
Every sigh becomes a hoot of cheer.

Resonance of the Resilient

In a realm where strong trees shake their hands,
And laughter echoes through the lands.
The wind tickles roots, oh what a thrill,
While shrubs sway dancing against their will.

A koala munches leaves, so aloof,
While critters ponder, what's their roof?
With each vigor born from stormy fight,
The flora form an impromptu fright!

"Let's throw a party!" the cuckoo sings,
As a beetle shows up wearing tiny blings.
The rustling leaves tap the beat along,
In nature's humor, they all belong.

Through trials, they giggle, roots intertwined,
With resilience wrapped in a punchline.
Even in struggles, they find their jest,
An ode to life, forever blessed.

Tides of Tenderness

As the waves of dusk wash the shores,
The trees giggle, a secret it pours.
With leaves that dance like they have no care,
Whispers float on, light as air.

Gentle breezes play with fading light,
While shadows tease, a silly sight.
The moon begins its silver strut,
And whispers to the puddles—a raucous rut.

The forest floor hums with a tune,
As fungi wobble beneath the moon.
Each step a squish, a joyous feel,
In this twilight dance, together they heal.

Through tides of change the laughter grows,
As each tale tails beneath the rose.
Here's to the giggles nature sends,
In every ending, a new trend bends.

Forgotten Canopy

In the woods where tall trees sway,
A koala snores the night away.
He dreams of leaves, a feast so grand,
But drools on branches—oh, what a stand!

The forest chuckles, trees in glee,
As bear belly shakes like a rough sea.
Caught in a snack, he starts to snore,
While echoes of laughter dance on the floor.

The Breath of Ancients

Ancient trees whisper tales of yore,
Of kangaroos who danced and swore.
With every breeze, they sigh in jest,
Like a dad joke from a well-earned rest.

A wombat waddles with great delight,
His antics turn day into night.
Nature's punchlines that never fade,
As legends in leaves are playfully made.

Fragrance of Lost Springs

Oh, the scent of springs long past,
A perfume that just couldn't last.
Moths whisper secrets, their wings quite bold,
While the trees share gossip from days of old.

A lizard grins with a twinkle in eye,
As insects zip and daringly fly.
They tease the roots, that wriggle with cheer,
Throwing shadows that giggle near.

Twilight in the Timber

Twilight falls, the sun slips down,
In the timber, joy wears a crown.
With shadows leaping, they play and prance,
Critters join in a twilight dance.

The light grows dim, but laughter rings,
As branches sway and the night owl sings.
With each hoot, the jokes take flight,
In this dimly lit, whimsical night.

When Giants Weep

A giant stood, his tears did flow,
Wishing on the leaves to grow.
He sighed aloud, what's my fate?
Join me, friend, let's contemplate.

With each gust, he swayed and moaned,
Falling leaves, the branches groaned.
"Why so gloomy?" I asked him quick,
"I lost my hat, that was the trick!"

The sun shined bright, the sky so blue,
He chuckled, shared a joke or two.
His bark was rough, but heart so light,
Together we laughed, feeling just right.

So if you see a giant cry,
Remember laughter's always nigh.
A tree with spirit, tall and grand,
In humor's shade, we take our stand.

Serenade of the Slender Stalks

In a grove, the slender stalks sway,
Whispering secrets of the day.
"We're here for fun!" they chirp in glee,
"Join our dance, just you and me!"

With tiny bows, they twist and bend,
A leafy party, where all pretend.
One leaf jumps, another spins,
"Don't be shy, let the swaying begin!"

The breeze brings jokes, they tumble free,
Tickling roots with silly glee.
"Why did the twig break out in song?
Because it knew it wouldn't be long!"

At dusk they rest, with giggles light,
The forest hums with pure delight.
Oh, to be among the green brigade,
Where every laugh is a leaf displayed!

Memory Lane in Green

Strolling down a leafy lane,
Memories dance, like sun and rain.
"Remember me?" a branch could say,
"I was your hat on that sunny day!"

Each rustle brings a tale to tell,
Of picnics and laughter, did you dwell?
A grove of friends, each tall and spry,
"Why not climb up?" they all reply.

One tree shimmies, twirls with pride,
"I wore a squirrel as a leafy guide!"
Laughter echoes, as they share,
Fleeting moments in the air.

With every giggle, a petal falls,
A memory caught, as nature calls.
So let's chase shadows, make some glee,
In the heart of green, just you and me!

The Saga of Swaying Leaves

In the wind, a tale unfolds,
Swaying leaves, their stories told.
"Ahoy there!" shouts a leaf so bright,
"Let's embark with all our might!"

They spin around, in happy plight,
Chasing shadows, hearts so light.
"What's a leaf's favorite game?"
"Falling down is the name of the fame!"

One leaf slipped, a graceful fall,
And in his wake, he called them all.
"Catch me quick, I'm on my way!
To the pile of laughs where we can play!"

As night approached, they settled down,
The wind was gently wearing a crown.
In every rustle, the laughter leaves,
A saga told among the eaves!

The Call of the Wild

In the forest thick with cheer,
The kookaburra holds court near.
It laughs so loud it shakes the leaves,
While nature nods and all believes.

A wallaby hops, such a sight!
With a bounce that takes off in flight.
But oh, those ants, they line up tight,
For a picnic feast—what a delight!

The trees all dance, they sway and shake,
As squirrels race for a nutty cake.
They trip and tumble, oh what fun!
In this wild realm, they can't be outdone.

A fan of feathers sings aloud,
With a swagger that would make you proud.
So join the troupe, it's plain to see,
The wild calls out, it's wild and free!

Embracing Solitude

In quiet moments, thoughts parade,
A lizard sunbathes, unafraid.
With a wink and blink, it catches flies,
While shadows dance under sunny skies.

A croc and turtle share a stare,
On a log, they lounge without a care.
In peace, they bask, with no one near,
A hermit's life, full of cheer!

The bumblebee bumbles, brimming bright,
A soloist in nature's light.
With a buzz, it claims its spot,
In this solo jam, it gives all it's got.

Though solitude brings quiet glee,
There's laughter lurking, wild and free.
Join the fun, don't shy away,
Embrace the peace, come out and play!

Cacophony of Fragrance

In the garden, scents collide,
Peppermint and citrus bide.
But who's that sneaking, oh so sly?
The skunk arises, and whoa, oh my!

Lavender whispers sweet and low,
While rosemary swirls in a fragrant flow.
Yet daisies giggle, petals a-light,
In this smell parade, there's pure delight!

A waft of garlic joins the fray,
Comedic chaos in olfactory play.
The flowers bloom, some twist and twirl,
As bees buzz in a fragrant whirl.

So raise your noses, take a whiff,
In this floral dance, don't you stiff.
Laugh along with scents so bold,
In this cacophony, stories unfold!

A Canopy of Calm

Beneath the trees, the world slows down,
A sloth meanders, wearing a crown.
Leaves flutter softly, they sip cool air,
While a wise old owl shows off flair.

The breeze is giggling through the boughs,
As creatures snooze and take their bows.
A turtle yawns, then snores out loud,
In this tranquil space where dreams are proud.

Sun-dappled secrets whisper low,
In shadows where the cool winds blow.
A playful breeze hums a lullaby,
While butterflies dance, oh my, oh my!

So find your peace in this lush retreat,
Where every heartbeat feels discreet.
With laughter hiding in nature's charm,
Welcome to the canopy of calm!

Dance of the Droplets

In the forest, raindrops prance,
Jumping here, they love to dance.
Each little splash, a giggling sound,
As puddles form up from the ground.

Misty hats on trees they wear,
Looking cute, beyond compare.
They twist and twirl in breezy play,
Making flowers laugh all day.

Each leaf whispers in pure delight,
Droplets sparkle, oh what a sight!
They bounce around like little sprites,
Underneath the silver lights.

So when you stroll through wooded paths,
Join the fun, don't miss the laughs.
For every drop has tales to tell,
In this dance, all is quite well.

Echoes of the Canopy

High above where treetops sway,
The leaves gossip in bright array.
Their chatter echoes, waves of cheer,
Telling secrets for all to hear.

Acorns tumble, squirrels rush,
While branches bend with a playful hush.
A parrot squawks, oh what a show,
As laughing winds through green leaves blow.

Birds in costumes, bright and bold,
Strike poses, so funny to behold.
The canopy, a stage set vast,
Where every creature plays a cast.

And down below, we can't help but smile,
At the antics going on awhile.
Laughter rings where shadows weave,
In this forest, let's believe!

Heartbeat of the Forest

Thump, thump, what do we hear?
It's the forest, full of cheer!
A heartbeat made of rustling leaves,
Funny things that nature weaves.

A deer jumps in, slips on a vine,
Trips and flops—oh, isn't that fine?
Frogs croak rhythms low and loud,
Creating laughter from a crowd.

Ants march in, a busily parade,
Their tiny feet in funny charade.
While woodpeckers knock in quirky time,
The forest's beat is pure sublime.

With each thud and flutter, we pulse as one,
In this crazy place, it's all just fun!
So listen close, and you will find,
Nature laughs—gently intertwined.

Beneath the Silvered Stalks

Beneath the stalks so tall and sleek,
Little critters peek and sneak.
With shiny smiles, they play their part,
In this comedy of nature's art.

Funny mushrooms in a row,
Telling tales that only they know.
The shadows dance, a wiggly spree,
Making goofs, just like you and me.

A hedgehog rolls, a tumble and spin,
His prickly coat, a laughable win.
While ladybugs play tag in a rush,
Their tiny giggles make a hush.

So come, find joy beneath the green,
Where laughter flows, and fun is seen.
In every nook, in every thrall,
Nature's humor pops for all!

Farewell to the Forest

The trees are dancing, oh what a sight,
But branches are waving goodbye tonight.
Their leaves are talking, in rustles and creaks,
Whispering secrets that nobody speaks.

A squirrel's thrown a party, nuts on the floor,
Raccoons are raving, can't ask for more!
They juggle the acorns like seasoned pros,
While owls roll their eyes at the silliness grows.

The bark's now a stage for the insects' ballet,
Ants in tuxedos stealing the day.
The forest's a mess, but who really cares?
With laughter and chaos spread through the bears!

But as we depart with a chuckle and grin,
The trees look on sadly, their party's begun.
We promise to visit, just don't shed a tear,
For the funny old forest will always be near.

Epiphany in the Emerald

Amidst the green whispers, a surprise so absurd,
A frog in a top hat, who croaks out a word.
He claims he's a prince, with a secret to tell,
While the beetles roll laughter, they know very well.

A butterfly winks, with a plan of escape,
To dance with the clouds, in a faraway shape.
But the daisies just giggle, insist on their space,
Saying, "Who needs the air when we've got this place?"

The sunlight's a spotlight, the laughter's the score,
As lizards breakdance and luminate folklore.
In the emerald sanctuary, no worries reside,
Just comedy gold, and a whimsical ride.

So here in this garden of emerald delight,
Life teaches us joy, even in the night.
In every location, look close and you'll see,
A moment of laughter, an epiphany free!

Anocean of Echoes

Down by the river, where the whispers convene,
Rabbits with surfboards, not quite serene.
They catch all the waves, with a hop and a flip,
The turtles just chuckle, pulling back a sip.

An otter's inquest, on a fish's career,
"Have you ever considered a change of sphere?"
The fish just giggles and dives out of sight,
Echoes of laughter twisting in light.

Bubbles are bursting with secrets and fun,
As crickets are DJing, from dusk till the sun.
The moon starts a wink, in glittery grace,
And all of the cosmos joins in the race.

In this ocean of echoes, absurdity reigns,
With a splash from the jesters, the laughter remains.
So let every ripple remind you to say,
Life's just a splash, let's laugh all the way!

Wistful Wind

The breeze pulls a prank, like a mischievous child,
 Tickling the ferns, making giggles go wild.
With whispers of stories, it flits through the trees,
 Collecting the laughter and buzzing with ease.

The leaves sway in rhythm, aware of the game,
While a caterpillar sighs, "Things never stay the same."
 Yet every gust carries a chuckle so near,
 Even the grumpy old pine cracks a cheer.

The wind tells of travels, of places unseen,
 Like a storyteller weaving with nature's routine.
With all of the creatures, they chirp in delight,
 Chasing the shadows as day turns to night.

So here's to the wind, with its whimsical streak,
 A companion in laughter, no need for a peak.
In the heart of the forest, where giggles are spun,
 We all find our joy, as the laughter's begun.

Symphony of the Silvers

In the forest, leaves do sway,
A tune of giggles come to play.
Branches dance in silly spins,
Whispers claim the trees are twins.

With every breeze, a chuckle's found,
The trunks all wear a merry frown.
Critters join in joyful song,
Nature's chorus, loud and strong.

Clouds above, a jolly crew,
Drifting dreams of wild bamboo.
Each falling leaf, a laugh out loud,
The woods are bright, the trees are proud.

And so the forest laughs away,
In this grand, absurd ballet.
Life's a jest, a forest game,
Under silver sky, we all exclaim!

Embrace of the Dusk

When twilight whispers soft and sweet,
The trees begin their funny feat.
With shadows long, they pull a face,
In that dusk's warm, glowing space.

A squirrel dons a cap so tall,
As crickets form a musical hall.
The night unfolds, a comic play,
While stars peek out to join the fray.

The moonlight winks, a playful tease,
As owls toast to the rustling leaves.
Each gust of wind, a laugh to share,
In this cheeky, evening air.

So let us sway in twilight's gold,
And dance through tales never told.
Nature's humor on full display,
In dusky light, we frolic and sway!

Cries of the Echoing Woods

In the woods where echoes play,
The trees have secrets, hip hooray!
Each gust a shout, a giggly tease,
Nature's joke on bumblebees.

The bushes mumble, squirrels jest,
In every nook, there's a wild fest.
Raccoons plotting with mischievous glee,
They dance in shadows near the free tree.

The laughter bounces, leaps, and soars,
While branches tickle all the floors.
The chirps and croaks, a humorous tune,
As daytime fades, and stars commune.

In this lively, echoing glade,
The woods assemble, and joy is made.
Every rustle has a tale to hum,
In this place where all things become!

Fragments of Forgotten Light

In the corners of the brightening gloom,
Dust motes dance, creating a room.
Fragments of light, so playful and spry,
Whisper to shadows as they drift by.

A flicker here, a glimmer there,
Each ray of laughter fills the air.
The garden's alive with grins and sighs,
As giggles echo 'neath the skies.

Through tangled vines, the sunbeams poke,
Telling tales in jests and yoke.
Each spark a tease, a prancing sprite,
In nature's dance of day and night.

So gather round, let's share our delight,
In fragments of glow, we take our flight.
For in this whimsical, gentle gleam,
Life's a comedy, a splendid dream!

Scented Shadows in the Breeze

In the park where leaves all sway,
The koalas snooze the day away.
With breaths that smell of minty gloom,
They plot the fate of tree and bloom.

A squirrel laughs, it leaps and flies,
In search of snacks, it's oh so sly.
The trees just giggle, roots entwined,
In whispered jokes, irony's kind.

When branches sway, the shadows dance,
Spinning tales of romance and chance.
The sunlight weaves through leafy frowns,
While nature sports its playful crowns.

Amidst the trunks, a rabbit grins,
Planning mischief, where fun begins.
With every rustle, joy seems to tease,
In this place of scented, swaying trees.

The Wailing Woods

In the woods where shadows creep,
The trees all moan, but none lose sleep.
They whisper tales both sad and sly,
    As birds above just flit and sigh.

A fox plays tricks, in jest, it prances,
While trees lament their lost romances.
Yet in their grief, there's humor found,
    With echoes of laughter all around.

The owls who hoot might join the show,
    As branches sway, putting on a pro.
    So much drama every night,
Who knew that trees could be so bright?

A flicker of light, a fleeting shade,
In this forest of jests, we're never afraid.
With wailing winds, the fun resumes,
    In the heart of these leafy tombs.

Song of the Silvery Trunks

The silver trunks hum a merry tune,
Under the watch of a lazy moon.
Swaying softly, they break into song,
While critters laugh and dance along.

A parrot squawks in a laugh-filled spree,
While the trees sway, full of glee.
Their limbs entwined, a jolly embrace,
Singing sweet nothings in every space.

The raccoons join in with a cheeky wink,
As the owls hoot and the crickets sync.
Their melody twirls on a gentle breeze,
Turning solemn nights into joyous tease.

So dance with me 'neath this star-lit coat,
With whispers of laughter, we shall float.
In harmony, we spin and prance,
In this serenade of leafy romance.

Ashen Memories

From ashes rise the sweetest dreams,
Where once there were trees in leafy schemes.
Now stumps hold stories of laughter lost,
Among the ghosts that dance at a cost.

They wink in time as the wind brings woes,
With chuckles of yore in each breeze that blows.
Mocking the past, they sway with grace,
In this realm of time and space.

Between gray barks, the humor grows,
As memories blossom where no one knows.
In the quiet night, jesters appear,
Recycling stories, bringing cheer.

So here we stand, beneath the gloom,
Among the shadows, we fit the room.
A comedy spun from tales of loss,
In ashen woods, we all become the gloss.

Song of the Wounded Timber

In the forest, I stand tall,
With a bark that does quite enthrall.
But alas, here comes a saw,
Making me feel quite raw.

The squirrels giggle, they know my plight,
I wiggle and dance, try to take flight.
With branches waving, a lumbering spree,
Oh, the irony, I'm still so free!

The birds tease me, 'you're losing your leaves!'
I chuckle back, 'oh, what a tease!'
While trees in suits mock my bare frame,
I'll spin in the wind, and dance just the same!

Once a giant, now a quirk,
In the lumberjack's eyes, I'm just a perk.
I laugh through the chainsaw's loud song,
In this leafy world, I simply belong.

Seasons of Solitude

Spring has sprung, but not on me,
I'm stuck in a patch of solitude, you see.
While others bloom, I just stand,
Giving shade to those in high demand.

Summer comes with a heatwave blast,
I'm feeling sticky, hoping it won't last.
The bugs throw parties on my trunk,
I just grin, pretty soon they'll sunk!

Autumn leaves dance, but none on my head,
I'm jealous of colors, and my bark feels dread.
The wind howls, they come and they go,
I shrug it off, I'm the star of my show!

Winter's near with a frosty bite,
Pine trees shout, 'look at our might!'
I chuckle and nod, dressed in my gray,
'At least I don't need a coat, hey hey!'

A Monologue of Mottled Trunks

Look at me, mottled and proud,
In this forest, I draw a crowd.
My stripes are unique, a true work of art,
Though some call me a tree with a funny heart.

I overhear whispers, 'he's got a style,'
I smile to myself, 'let's stay for a while.'
The sap drips down like my own tear,
Yet I stand resilient, never fear!

The owls come by for their nightly chat,
I tell them jokes, and they hoot with a spat.
While the pines grow tall and think they're the best,
I'm here with my comedy, putting them to rest!

So if you wander by, stop for a tale,
Join me beneath where the squirrels prevail.
With chuckles and laughter, forget all your woes,
In this groovy trunk world, anything goes!

The Last Dance of the Tall Ones

In the twilight, the tall ones sway,
With limbs flapping like they want to play.
'Look at me!' one shouts with glee,
'Bet you can't dance like me!'

The sun dips low, it's our final waltz,
We shimmy and shake with no faults.
The branches tangle, a comical sight,
As the stars twinkle and join the delight.

The wind blows in, with a playful shove,
Sending us spinning, like we've fallen in love.
The moon giggles and rolls on the floor,
With each twist and turn, we ask for more!

As the night fades and the dawn takes flight,
We chuckle softly: 'What a night, alright!'
Though we're giants, we still know the game,
To dance with a smile, and never feel shame.

Beneath the Blue-Hued Boughs

Under boughs so blue and bright,
Koalas snore with all their might.
They dream of leaves and heavenly snacks,
While we sip tea and wonder the facts.

A squirrel dashes, just a blur,
Waving his tail, a furry stir.
He steals a leaf, oh what a thief!
We laugh, then sigh, it's beyond belief!

Beneath branches that sway and creak,
Nature whispers, jokes so cheek.
A breeze tickles, makes us grin,
As birds crack jokes, oh where to begin?

So let's dance below this leafy dome,
With laughter echoing, we feel at home.
Every giggle floats on the air,
Under boughs that just don't care.

Layers of Time

In layers of time, the leaves do fall,
We gather them up, a colorful haul.
A history written in flecks of green,
With stories of critters, oh, what a scene!

The bark peels away, revealing the past,
Of forest nights and breezes vast.
We play hide and seek in the shadows cast,
While the sun shines down, a bright contrast.

A squirrel's doing the cha-cha slide,
While ants march in a silly pride.
They don't know it, but they bring us cheer,
As we gaze up with a giggle and a jeer.

So layer by layer, it's laughter we find,
In the chaotic chaos that nature designed.
With every rustle, a joke or a rhyme,
We doodle our dreams on this canvas of time.

Lost in Petals and Bark

Lost amidst petals, I trip and fall,
A clumsy tumble, but isn't life a ball?
The flowers giggle, their colors ablaze,
As bees buzz by, in a nectar craze.

The bark stands firm, with stories untold,
Of chattering critters, both brave and bold.
Yet here I am, in a flower child's dream,
Collecting giggles, like ice cream.

A kookaburra laughs up in the tree,
At my antics, oh can't you see?
Nature's audience, they all applaud,
While I dance like a dodo, this cheeky facade.

So let Petals be my dance floor tonight,
As I twirl and tumble, merry and light.
With a bouquet of giggles, I'll take my mark,
In a world so bright, I won't miss the spark.

The Stillness Between Storms

In stillness found between the noise,
A lull where nature lets out its joys.
Leaves rustle softly, a secret shared,
While squirrels meditate, oh they are prepared!

The sky's a canvas, painted in grey,
But laughter brews in its own little way.
A raindrop teases, then splashes the ground,
While frogs croak jokes, bubbling around.

Amidst the calm before the fun,
We spot a rainbow, oh what a run!
Chasing colors, we dance in delight,
As shadows prepare for a zip and a flight.

So let's revel in this playful hour,
Beneath tree canopies that give us power.
In the stillness, let laughter bloom,
For nature's comedy dispels all gloom.

Enigma of the Edges

A tree in a hat, so proud and so tall,
Whispers of spice in a green carpet hall.
Branches like arms waving hello,
What secrets they hold, only they truly know.

Leaves have a giggle, the sun starts to shine,
Dancing like dancers, oh what a design!
Breeze tells a joke, they all start to sway,
All in good humor, who needs to be gray?

Squirrels in bow ties, acorns in tow,
Planning a party, the grandest of shows.
Chatting of winter, of summer's delight,
Hoping for laughter all through the night.

So here's to the trees, with their whimsical ways,
Bringing us chuckles and sunny bright days.
In shadows they plot, in sunlight they play,
Nature's own comedy, come join the fray!

Veil of the Verdant

In the land of the green, oh what do we see?
A shrub wearing glasses, sipping sweet tea.
Frogs in tuxedos, trading their bets,
Betting on raindrops and get-rich regrets.

Laughter erupts from the roots down below,
As daisies tell secrets to thorns, oh the show!
A dance in the wind, not a care in the world,
Pollen confetti, as petals are twirled.

Chirping of birds in full comedic flair,
Mimicking humans, they're quite the rare pair.
"Who needs an umbrella?" a clump of weeds cheer,
"When you are as brave as a buck with no fear?"

The breeze is a jokester, teasing each day,
Spreading the laughter, come join in the play.
Amidst leafy laughter, the sun starts to laugh,
Life's but a comedy, just look at the track!

Poetry of the Pillars

Tall as a tower, they reach for the skies,
Whispering tales with their wrap-around lies.
A trunk full of jokes, the bark is a quip,
You'd think they were drunk with each playful dip.

In shadows they gather, gossip flows free,
"Did you hear the one about the old apple tree?"
"Oh, that cracked me up!" chuckles a stout willow,
While the oaks just grin, being quite the tight fellow.

Karaoke night with the wind as the judge,
As branches sing out in a comedic grudge.
"Not bad for a pine!" yells a goofy old birch,
"Though I'd trade my needles for a seat in the church!"

So here's to the pillars of green in our midst,
Where laughter is timeless and hope can't be missed.
With every small breeze, a chuckle ignites,
In the heart of the forest, where humor ignites!

Tapestry of Time

Rugged and twisted like a comical thread,
The boughs weave a canvas where laughter is bred.
A tapestry bright with the colors of mirth,
It sings to the critters, it tickles the earth.

Vines long and winding, in hats made of dew,
All fashion their whims with bright bows and a shoe.
"Did you hear the one about the sloth in a suit?"
His clients were leaves, oh how they took root!

A patchwork of giggles sprinkles the ground,
When the clouds share their cream, it's silliness found.
Together they scheme for the next sunny spout,
Chasing the rain with a jovial shout.

So dance with the leaves, let the joy take its course,
In the timeless embrace of this humor-filled force.
Weaving each moment with jokes yet unsaid,
In the fabric of nature, where laughter is fed!

Whispers of the Silver Leaves

In the breeze, leaves joke and sway,
Telling tales of their silly day.
One leaf claims it slipped in tea,
But others just laugh, as leaves agree.

They gather round like friends at night,
Spinning yarns in soft moonlight.
A bird flew by, said birds this year,
Are surely the silliest, oh dear!

The branches creak, their laughter loud,
As insects gather, wondering how.
For every drop of dew that falls,
A leaf cracks jokes and sheer childish brawls.

Yet when the sun begins to rise,
Their secrets fade under azure skies.
Hope they remember, in leafy jest,
That laughing leaves know how to rest.

In the Shade of the Lonesome Tree

There stands a tree with arms so wide,
But all it does is sit and hide.
Befriended by squirrels, a nutty crew,
They call him Steve; he's feeling blue.

He sighs and bends, a whimsical frown,
While birds above chirp, dance and clown.
"Oh, to be light, like you guys in flight,"
But still he stands, a noteworthy sight.

One day a bee hums with a sting,
"Join us down here, it's a buzzing thing!"
But Steve just sways, sticks out a limb,
"Thanks for the invite, but I'm too dim!"

As shadows stretch in the setting sun,
He pockets dreams of relishing fun.
Perhaps tomorrow, he'll shed his gloom,
Get up, get down, weave through the room!

Ghosts of the Gumtree Grove

In the grove where shadows linger,
Sway the ghosts, and snap their finger.
Telling tales of lost bark and leaves,
With punchlines that dance like autumn eaves.

"I once was tall, proud with a crown,
But a storm came by, and I tumbled down!"
One ghost sighed, with a cheeky grin,
"At least I've got roots, I can still spin!"

They recall their youth, whooshing with glee,
"We swayed so hard, we set the world free!"
A wandering breeze throws a sarcastic shout,
"You're all just swayed by what's around about!"

Yet in the moonlight, their laughter soars,
In ghostly forms, they open new doors.
Among the trees, the stories weave,
And even ghosts know how to believe!

Melancholy in the Mist

A fog rolled in, dressed in gray,
Whispering secrets of long gone play.
Beneath the cover, a branch did droop,
A sad little tree, lost in its loop.

"It's just my luck," it grumbled low,
"While others dance, I'll put on a show!"
The leaves giggled, holding breath so tight,
As raindrops fell, a whimsical sight.

A squirrel jumped, saying, "Cheer up, friend!
Your leafy tales do not have to end!"
But the trunk just sighed, in moody defeat,
"Without the light, it's hard to compete!"

Yet in the mist, a chuckle broke free,
"Who knew sadness was so spry and free?"
With every droplet sparkling with bliss,
The tree laughed loud; it found its twist.

Memories of the Breezy Glade

In the glade where green trees dance,
Leaves whisper tales of a squirrel's prance.
With branches tickling the sunlit air,
They giggle at ants, unaware of their flair.

A koala dreams, arms stretched wide,
Hoping his lunch won't take a ride.
While cicadas sing a buzzing tune,
They make the sun feel like a cartoon.

Lively breezes tease the grass,
Forgetting the time will surely pass.
Amid the laughter of nature's jest,
Each creature welcomes a noonday rest.

But banter stops with a woeful sigh,
As playful shadows stretch and lie.
Still, we chuckle at the leafy show,
In this glade where the breezes blow.

Reverie of the Forest Floor

Ferns are hats for mushrooms below,
In this jumbled world, oh, what a show!
Worms sport sunglasses beneath the shade,
While beetles trade tales of their escapade.

A rabbit hops with rhythmic grace,
Chasing a butterfly in a silly race.
While grasshoppers leap like tiny glee,
Laughing as frogs join in with tea.

The ground is a stage where all can prance,
Each leaf a ticket to this wild dance.
Amid the chaos, giggles ignite,
Under the canopy, all feels just right.

Yet, amid this cheer, a gentle poke,
From a hedgehog who just wants to joke.
Life is a romp in this forest grand,
Where all creatures play, hand in hand.

Shadows of Silhouette

Shadows waltz as the sun grows low,
Swirling freely in a twilight glow.
An owl winks, casting cheeky doubts,
As drowsy dreams awaken sprightly shouts.

The silhouettes of foxes prance,
Beneath the moon, they take their chance.
Chasing their tails with gleeful glee,
While wishing on stars—they giggle with glee.

Branches stretch like arms of delight,
Tickling the stars that blink at night.
In this blurry world of silky gray,
Even the shadows dare to play.

Yet soon it fades, this silly bout,
And all the laughter begins to pout.
But they'll return when the sun is set,
In shadows where joy and whimsy met.

Tears Among the Tall Ones

Among the tall ones, a droplet falls,
A tree sobs as a bird recalls.
He misses the days of juvenile fun,
When he danced with the ground and kissed the sun.

The branches weep in a leafy decree,
With rustling sighs like a lost bumblebee.
Yet a parrot squawks, 'Hold that thought!'
'Life's too silly for all this rot!'

Still, the leaves shake with bittersweet glee,
As raccoons prance, wild and free.
They cheer for the tears from the sky so wide,
Claiming the rain is just nature's ride.

And with a chuckle, the tall ones sway,
Finding humor in a rainy day.
For even amidst the sobs and sighs,
There's laughter hidden beneath the skies.

www.ingramcontent.com/pod-product-compliance
Lightning Source LLC
Chambersburg PA
CBHW071815160426
43209CB00003B/93